M000284607

Walt McDonald
Selected Poems

TCU Press

Fort Worth, Texas

TCU Texas Poet Laureate Series

COPYRIGHT © 2016 BY WALT MCDONALD

Library of Congress Cataloging-in-Publication Data

Names: McDonald, Walter, author.
Title: Selected poems / Walt McDonald.
Other titles: TCU Texas poet laureate series.
Description: Fort Worth, Texas : TCU Press, [2016] | Series: TCU Texas poet
    laureate series
Identifiers: LCCN 2016017437 (print) | LCCN 2016018135 (ebook) | ISBN
    9780875656342 (alk. paper) | ISBN 9780875656458
Subjects: LCSH: Texas--Poetry. | Texas, West--Poetry. | Southwestern
    States--Poetry.
Classification: LCC PS3563.A2914 A6 2016 (print) | LCC PS3563.A2914
(ebook) |
    DDC 811/.54--dc23
LC record available at https://lccn.loc.gov/2016017437

TCU Press
P.O. Box 298300
Fort Worth, TX 76129
817.257.7822
www.prs.tcu.edu

To order books: 1.800.826.8911

Designed by fusion29
www.fusion29.com

FOR RILEY JANE AND AMELIA SCOUT

WITH LOVE—POPS

01

contents

Introduction

Walt McDonald was named Texas State Poet Laureate in 2001. TCU Press honors his amazing career in this tenth book of the TCU Press Texas Poet Laureate Series.

For this editor, the most difficult part of putting this book together was choosing from his many incredible poems. Walt McDonald has been one of my favorite poets since the first time I read him, years ago. Still today, I never travel without at least one of his twenty-two books tucked into my bag.

His work moves me on an elemental level, inspiring memories and ideas that ignite my own poetry like sparks from an anvil. He is one I reach for when going into that temple of writing. I read his work, and my own work flows.

McDonald was first introduced to poetry in grade school with a visit from the third Texas Poet Laureate, Grace Noll Crowell, to his Lubbock classroom. This is the power of the Texas Poet Laureate; indeed the very reason for this laureate series. Perhaps with McDonald, it began there. All it takes is one inspired student, and poetry takes root in the next generation.

Walt McDonald began his writing career in fiction, working on his first novel during his senior year at Texas Tech University. He stayed at Tech for his master's degree while awaiting entry into pilot training. He attended the US Air Force Academy, then shipped off to Iowa where he received his PhD in 1966.

He is the author of twenty collections of poems listed on the acknowledgments page of this book. His *Great Lonely Places of the Texas Plains* pairs poems with color photos by Texas State Photographer Wyman Meinzer. *Whatever the Wind Delivers: Celebrating West Texas and the Near Southwest*, which won a Western Heritage Award from the National Cowboy Hall of Fame, includes archival photos selected by Janet Neugebauer from Tech's Southwest Collection, as does *All That Matters: The Texas Plains in Photographs and Poems*. He has also published a book of fiction, *A Band of Brothers: Stories from Vietnam* (1989).

McDonald came to poetry late in life, as a middle-aged air force pilot turning to poems as a way of "saying things that couldn't be said any other way," as he put it. "After some of my friends went off to Vietnam, and one was shot down, then another," he said, "I felt a need to say something to them or about them." Soon he became well known for *Band of Brothers* and for *After the Noise of Saigon*, his poetry about the war. One such poem from *Faith is a Radical Master* is titled "For Friends Missing in Action:"

Often, I've caught a glint of silver,
fliers trusting their dials and wing tips.

Odd, walking flat sand after years in a cockpit,
caught between the earth and angels. How many loops

and barrel rolls, thrusting from earth
inverted, how many dives and pull-outs,

straining to stop blood rushing from my skull.
I see young pilots on TV, faces lined

from their masks, cropped hair and ancient eyes,
the stance of tigers. I remember Millard

and Roy Carnes shot down in jungle,
Bob Ross and Jones, and Billy Ray Moegle,

the squadron clown, dragged through Hanoi,
still missing—fellows on fire with laughter,

God on our side through any skies we dared,
the future paved with runways leading home.

A master of the story, the subtle rhythm of the line, this prolific poet has had more than 2,300 poems published in journals. McDonald served as poetry editor for Texas Tech University Press from 1975 to 1995 and re-tired in May 2002 as Paul Whitfield Horn Professor of English and Poet in Residence at Texas Tech. He was a member of the literature advisory panel for the Texas Commission on the Arts (1986-88).

McDonald won four Western Heritage Awards from the National Cowboy Hall of Fame and six awards from the Texas Institute of Letters, including the Lon Tinkle Memorial Award for Excellence Sustained Throughout a Career. He also received the Bookend Award for a lifetime of contributions to Texas literature from Texas Tech University Press in 2004.

Even those with no knowledge of his many accolades remain moved by his words. McDonald's poems seem to rise up from the soil and all the earthly waters, ripe with wisdom, connecting one generation to the next: the sweet meat of a fictional history handed down to the rest of the world with the splendor of the grand storytellers of the past. In his poem, "Aunt Linda and the Pink Bikini," he puts the reader in the family living room, chair-to-chair with each character. (A note to the reader: in that era, "thongs" referred to flip-flops.) The poem begins:

Her tongue was spice and lightning . . . .

Men liked her summer laugh,
pink thongs and terry cloth. I remember Aunt Linda
in bikinis at picnics, divorced in-law, but family.

I was bold with mustard for her burgers,
the perfect nephew. Linda always had a sticky kiss
for me, and whispered six-packs of advice—"Shave close
and take no prisoners." She clipped me on the chin
and left sweet lipstick on my cheek.

McDonald's capacity for detail is remarkable, capturing human interaction and inflection as only a trained observer can. "Every poem is personal," McDonald said in an interview with Chris Ellery in 1995, "but every poem is also a persona poem, a little fiction." It is this fact that is most surprising to the reader—left in total belief that McDonald, who currently lives in Lubbock, Texas, with his wife Carol, rode the West Texas range all these years; branded thousands of cattle; shot, cooked, and ate rattlesnakes; suffered the ranchers' drought; and learned the cattleman's lessons from his dozens of grandfathers, aunts and uncles, such as in the poem "Uncle Earl's Last Ride in Dallas":

Uncle Earl's blue suit hung like a rustler's,
four pairs of boots lined up like a posse's
in the closet. We did what we must
with a will's stipulation—Levi's
and long-sleeved shirt unbuttoned,
his best beaver Stetson, back brim cut flush

to let his head lie flat. A chaw of Red Man
in his jaws, stitched tight and natural . . .

His poems are intense and deep, able to summon up life and death in just a few stanzas with expertly placed line breaks. McDonald is master of the poetic white space, something he thinks all poets would benefit in learning. "I still believe it's worth it when I find a poem that makes me love what matters in this world," McDonald said. "Writing a poem is simply taking something you know—something everyone knows—and singing about it in your own way."

McDonald is a regionalist, no doubt, but his poems swim in the everyday life of places as diverse as Texas, Vietnam, Montana, and Colorado. Sense of place is crucial in his work, and as Ellery said, just as Robert Frost's was New England and Eudora Welty's was Mississippi, Walt McDonald's place seems to be centered most in the unapologetic fangs of West Texas—beautiful in its ferocity.

Through his work, we see man, not at odds with his unyielding world, but accepting: Stetson pulled low, cinching the saddle tighter; all his weight on a horse named Faith, as in "Praying For Rain On The Plains":

If it comes,
let tractors stall hub-deep.
Pull off your boots and walk without socks,
squeeze globs of what you are. Feel mud like Vaseline,
the crushed and processed ferns and dinosaurs.
In a million years, we'll ooze from vaults
and metal caskets, back in the mud where we belong. . . .

But, as in all great writers, regionalism is only the bounce of the diving board. McDonald takes us from his own region up to a universal world, where we dive down along beside him into the depths of our own memories; into far deeper emotions. This is the crux of good poetry, when readers draw their own meanings, their own needs from the poems. "When writers accept their regions," McDonald said, "they plug into their own motherlode of images. Until they do, they simply miss the obvious—the uniqueness of place, the abundant reservoir of images, details, and insights that matter most to them."

And, it is in these images that he shows us why poetry is essential in our lives.

Every poet strives for this type of connection with the reader, and Walt McDonald does it in simple but powerful language, the readers finding themselves out of breath at the end of each poem, not realizing they had held it.

karla k. morton

Guest Editor, TCU Texas Poet Laureate Series

With special thanks and acknowledgment to Chris Ellery for his "Interview with Walt McDonald," (1995) and to the Poetry Foundation, publisher of *Poetry* Magazine.

Acknowledgments

The poems in this collection, some of which were previously published in slightly different versions, were selected from the following volumes:

Splitting Wood for Winter (University of North Texas Press, 1988)

Rafting the Brazos (University of North Texas Press, 1988)

Night Landings (Harper, 1989)

All That Matters: The Texas Plains in Photographs and Poems, photographs selected by Janet M. Neugebauer (Texas Tech University Press, 1992)

Where Skies Are Not Cloudy (University of North Texas Press, 1993)

Blessings the Body Gave (Ohio State University Press, 1998)

Whatever the Wind Delivers: Celebrating West Texas and the Near Southwest, photographs selected by Janet M. Neugebauer (Texas Tech University Press, 1999)

All Occasions (University of Notre Dame, 2000)

Climbing the Divide (University of Notre Dame, 2003)

Great Lonely Places of the Texas Plains, photographs by Wyman Meinzer (Texas Tech University Press, 2003)

A Thousand Miles of Stars (Texas Tech University Press, 2004)

Faith is a Radical Master: New and Selected Poems (ACU Press, 2005)

Some of the poems were previously published in periodicals:

Poetry Magazine, 1987: "Losing a Boat on the Brazos"

Cowboy Poetry: The Reunion, Virginia Bennett and Charlie Seemann, 2004: "Old Pets"

"Poetry and Medicine." *JAMA: Journal of the American Medical Association* 285: No. 9 (2001): 1128. Copyright 2001, American Medical Association.

Walt McDonald's other poetry collections include: *Counting Survivors; After the Noise of Saigon; The Flying Dutchman; Caliban in Blue and Other Poems; Anything, Anything; Burning the Fence; Working against Time;* and *Witching on Hardscrabble.*

GOATS IMPORTED FROM AUSTIN

Goats stumbled on shale, a rocky mesa
Daddy fenced for kids imported from Austin.
He swore *cabrito* would be worth the smell,
a market killing, but hated goats—

cattle the only odor for a man. Coyotes and rattlers
roamed those acres until he claimed them.
Goats climbed the hill like bighorn sheep,
playing king of the mountain, bold on the bluff,

staring at greener pastures. Other goats popped up
like penguins, searching for all he saw in the distance.
My brother and I fed goats by hand, lugged oats
to kids with nubbin horns, bellies that bulged

and muscles butting us for buckets. After chores,
we dragged our wagons to the top. Where the cliff
dropped off, we risked the bumpy ride downhill,
tumbling, bending the wheels and tongues.

The goats ignored us, picking their paths
up and down like angels. After frost,
our father slaughtered them all and hung them
one by one from rafters, smoking the meat

for winter, the market for cattle and goats
collapsed, the start of the Texas depression.
Drinking windmill water to swallow,
we chewed tough jerky for years,

salt-cured and stringy. We learned to curse
the dust of a ranch that failed
and played field hockey without a stick,
kicking the tiny hoofs like pucks.

ALL THE OLD SONGS

I never knew them all, just hummed
and thrummed my fingers with the radio,
driving a thousand miles to Austin.
Her arms held all the songs I needed.
Our boots kept time with fiddles
and the charming sobs of blondes,

the whine of steel guitars
sliding us down in deer-hide chairs
when jukebox music was over.
Sad music's on my mind tonight
in a jet high over Dallas, earphones
on channel five. A lonely singer,

dead, comes back to beg me,
swearing in my ears she's mine,
rhymes set to music which make
complaints seem true. She's gone
and others like her, leaving their songs
to haunt us. Letting down through clouds

I know who I'll find tonight at home,
the same woman faithful to my arms
as she was those nights in Austin
when the world seemed like a jukebox,
our boots able to dance forever,
our pockets full of coins.

THE LAST GOOD SADDLES

We've worked these plains so long we're broke.
Two old neighbors can't make the dust feed calves
forever. August this hot makes yucca
drop its pods, snakes hibernate till dark,

horned owls believe they're wise,
grasping the limbs of live oaks.
Black buzzards glide, patrolling all we own.
Wherever they swirl, coyotes are sure to follow,

starving for cow bones broken,
tumbled down steep arroyos. Soon,
we'll round up strays enough to drive
to two corrals, brands on their flanks

better than fences to keep two fools
from quarrels—this calf is mine;
that, yours, the brittle grass they find
on open range good to be chewed over and over.

Rolling a smoke the old way, we listen to thunder,
the distant rumble of rain. Too late
to do much good this season even if it floods.
You spit, and wipe a stiff glove over stubble.

Buzzards seem fatter than these steers.
But let's go, coaxing our sorrels back
between mesquite and cactus, the simple oats
they work for at least enough for them.

Tonight at the campfire we'll sip cold beer
and quarrel about taxes and the price of bulls,
about drought and stalled squall lines,
about whose old bones first felt the rain.

MIDNIGHT near PECOS

Last night, camped in a tent in a clearing,
I heard the storm die down in time
to hear wolves running, a deer
splashing through dry stalks

of the grain field, crashing downwind
and dying, the pack claiming their right
to fields I've leased for hunting.
I felt my old pig heart grab like a fist,

wanting them all, *my deer, mine,*
I felt the hair on my neck rise up
like pig bristles. I'd gone to market
for these deer-rifle bullets and boots.

I huffed and cursed and dared any wolves
to try blowing down my tent.
I'd fire point-blank, slaughter the pack
and make deer safe for hunters like me

for years. Mad as a boar, I lay back down
and snarled and fell asleep grunting
and rooting around in the sleeping bag
for my socks, my human feet.

COAT COLLARS UP LIKE THUGS

When Marva wobbled, boys parted like the sea.
Her sandals crossed like a model's
when she walked, controlled crash of hips

and blouse already thick. Marva was a marvel
of biology, classmate of skinny boys in love.
At recess, we shoved each other

off the monkey bars, defying the safety rules
and steps, climbing the slick, steep slide.
If Marva came to the playground

I don't recall. We thought she might
and that was enough for fistfights and quarrels,
knives in our pockets never opened, but almost.

She was a dish, a dimpled Shirley Temple at thirteen.
Mid-term, when Marva moved, the gang went silent.
We slouched until the recess bell and scowled

at silly first graders across the street
teasing each other on swings. Flicking cigarettes
we stole from our mothers, we trudged back

to brown steel doors, coat collars up like thugs,
checking out the fire escape, which room
it was close to, how many feet to the ground.

Aunt Emma and the Spoils of War

When she found the herd bull dead,
Aunt Emma said *Now everything makes sense*.
She accepted when the pastor was fired,
when cattle went up five cents,

when my mother's appendix burst.
Every success and death, she shook her head,
another worry bead for her rosary—
her husband's jungle rot, the long Pacific war,

the Bomb. We're thread in the eye of a needle,
she believed, beasts in a fable called fate.
I saw the grainy photograph of her as a bride
in the hall, red-lipped laughing girl

of sixteen, weeks after Pearl Harbor.
After the honeymoon, Uncle Roy shipped out.
She swore she'd die childless if he died
in combat. After the land mine

flattened him, she swore he wouldn't die.
They shipped him back, patched up and whole
except what mattered most to him.
Aunt Emma taught him the rhythm

of rocking chairs and cards, helped him
until he could ride a horse without flinching.
She talked adoption, brought the first
blind child back home in her arms

while Uncle Roy drove, tight-jawed
and tall as a stallion. For years, I watched him romp
with his kids, five orphans everyone loved—
big-grin, clumsy cousins who hugged

and clung to Uncle Roy, mellow as Emma's jam.
Aunt Emma set extra plates for my sister and me
on visits, humming, counting children like beads
and nodding, now that everything made sense.

one summer before saigon

That August, I came with Ursula to the tomb,
ducking under marble archways to the wall.
Ivy tangled down, coiled like snakes
chasing their tails. Blonde Ursula
without a bra, silk blouse unbuttoned
to the breast bone—what would Uncle Joe
have said to that? Say *Holy nipples, girl,*

say *Hug old Uncle Joe.* That year,
I defied Aunt Peggy's frown, *Behold,*
the hussy comes. Childless, Uncle Joe
had left me his ranch, his Purple Heart
and Silver Star, his cattle and stallions.
And so that morning after communion, I took her
to the tomb for Uncle Joe's amusement,

knowing Aunt Peggy would sneer and scoff
inside pink marble, would have boxed his cheeks
with both big-diamonded fists. *Down, you lecher,*
down! She'd know we had come from church
where Ursula gave sweet tongue to the bishop,
who balked and laid the wafer there—
that naked tongue, tight blouse confessing flesh.

All that, one crazy summer before Saigon,
the savage meat I needed. Before port call
and the long flight overseas, I spent
last nights in a bedroll, as far from war
as cattle in pastures of coyotes,
calm in the dark by my campfire
under the hottest stars there are.

Anniversary Waltz

On the stairs, near the top of the stairs,
she waited like a sweetheart in a cheap
soap-opera scene, and me the maverick come back.
Ursula played the heiress beset by every suntanned Tad
and Biff mad for a looker like her in scenes like that.

That day it might have been Biff or Lance
with a shiny tie, holding a program for her
at the opera in Austin, already distant from him
and focused on me, wild for her amazing lipstick
and hair, yes, and her tiny waist in that black dress.

What was a pilot in town for the weekend to do
after she had gone off to college and me half-mad
to Saigon, dog-fighting day and night
in bars and foreign skies? I attacked
two stairs at a time, always the clown, half-Joseph,

half-Romeo to her one of a kind—*Behold,*
my leap and shuffle said, *this dreamer comes.*
And she, blue-eyed and dazzling, unhooked and tugged
at her left glove, then let me take her hand,
both hands, and it was true, she had no ring.

After giddy hellos and hugs, after the opera started
and the lobby cleared and it was obvious
even to ushers she was the mother-to-be
of our children—grimly, digging for cigarettes,
Biff or Lance went down the stairs.

BUZZarDS anD UnCLe DOUGLaS

Uncle Douglas taught his dogs to chase off
buzzards in the sky. He cursed their black apparel,
their bowed necks praying for the dead.
He wanted them starved above his dying trees.
Saplings died faster than he could haul them off,

nothing but lumber in his heart after Aunt Wanda died.
Douglas was a pharaoh of dying aspens, without a son.
Fungus killed all aspens on his farm, nothing to do
but cut them. He dropped his chain saw down
and stacked them, his skies haunted by a slow

whirlpool of wings. The old man loved those dogs
but never let strangers see him pet them,
never mind the moon, the nights we fished together,
the lake trout fighting for their lives. He taught me
the feel of mud underfoot, the way to cast

far out for lunkers. He hated anything that grieved
in public. From his woodlot we watched them
like a black mobile of mourners that never cared
for something while it lived. He cursed them all,
an old man lost in a forest who hated every day

he wasted while Aunt Wanda lived. Gruff, he taught me
to sit so still I heard stars burning. In August,
he harnessed the mule and let the road to the depot
keep us both from choking, holding me tight as a son
before my train pulled out.

MY BrOTHer anD THE GOLDen GLOVes

My body knew the bold flurry of his fists.
Twelve and fifteen, we grew up brothers
in different worlds. He had scars
I knew made him a hero
though he hated fights,

the Golden Gloves our daddy's idea.
Boys pretending to be tough
stopped by, smoking their butts,
crushing them in our grass.
After they left, dried blood

stuck to his fists, the bridge of his nose.
Korea was almost lost when he enlisted.
I remember his fist in his hair
when he came home, as if he'd lost his comb.
He crushed cigarettes in ashtrays,

tried odd jobs and quit them.
I asked about the war, how many friends
he lost. He turned away as if to save me,
his right hand always a fist. Our father
gave him the car and sold the fatted calf

and gave him that to hold him.
I remember gravel pinging
the family sedan, I remember our father
alone in the street with a billfold,
waving *come back* and crying.

COYOTES AND DOGS

Uncle Earl kept a Saint Bernard in his tavern
before the state law banned it, the patron dog
of his dance hall. My knuckles knew his rubber lips,
his purple tongue, thick double chins stuffed with fur.
He clung like a python when I scratched him,

digging my fist in his ribs. Cowboys taught him
to howl sad tunes with the jukebox. Girls tossed him
quarters, the only dog on the dance floor,
waddling past couples locked in each other's arms.
Lapping draft beer, he lay down by blondes

and cowboys who tugged off leather gloves
and let him lick stiff knuckles busted in rodeos.
Fists that shot wild dogs and coyotes
burrowed into folds of fur and made
his massive paw keep time, thumping the floor.

I remember how he howled and tugged outside
after the sheriff left, the moon no jukebox,
a dozen pickups but not one fist to pet him,
sniffing packs of coyotes miles away,
dragging the stiff chain tight.

on taking a grandson hunting

Only later, as he approached
expecting nothing breathing
in feathers he aimed at,

but something flat like pelts
on highways—fearing no evil.
At least with its eyes closed.

And most lay still.
Woodcarvings.
Nothing like doves.

In his sleeping bag in the camper
all night he tried to forget
the one dove bleeding

with eyes like a kitten,
the throat rapidly beating,
the dark pearls.

GELDINGS ON MOUNTAIN RANCHES

Horses in barns survive the cold on oats
trucked up from town, vacation from tourists
who pay to kick their ribs in spring
and jerk them nervously on trails.

Switchbacks a thousand feet straight down
are nothing to geldings lifting bristled tails.
They pass stale gas to each other like code,
clopping iron shoes single file up mountains

one hoof at a time. Climbing is all they do
under tight-lipped people they'll never save again.
They take two extra steps before turning, the gasps
and squeezing knees well worth the jolt of bits

twisting them back from the edge, uphill.
They know how close to the ledge they can go,
how many times before the wrangler scolds them.
If they remember loping green pastures,

the bucking days before castration, hay muzzles them
after a day of trails, stroking their tongues over oats.
They never nod for strangers patting their rumps,
Nice horse. Tourists smooth their necks and whisper

Sweetheart, digging in tight Levi's for sugar cubes
crushed to powder, grateful to be alive after cliffs
where they might have died but for these steeds,
these massive, muscled legs.

THE SECOND TIME AROUND

If by some tide I had found you strolling,
holding white sandals by the thongs,
what could I have done, assuming someone
husbandly held your other hand like a pearl?

When you said no and flew away, I let you go,
what else? For months, I bored holes
in thunderclouds, flung a jet boldly
over fields and forests, pulled hard

and corkscrewed up at the sun, the wild blue,
not even hoping. Women from Georgia to Hawaii
danced softly in my arms, fondling my silver wings.
Not one of them was you. And then that noon

of now-done longing when I turned and saw you
there on the stairs, staring at me across the hall
before the opera started, startled to find you again,
alone, without a ring, and coming down the stairs.

THE WINTER OUR GRANDSON TURNED THIRTEEN

When I open both fists wide, my God!
what wrinkles, like a pond rippled
on a windy day, seen from a thousand feet
in a chopper. Squeezed into fists again,
the skin tries to lie about my age,
betrayed by creases like canals on Mars.

I've seen these hands on Grandfather
in the hospital, an IV needle
taped like a tire patch, my hero
who carved hawks and robins from blocks
of mahogany and oak, feathers so real
I swore he could make the buffed wood fly.

How fast my skimpy lifeline aged
in these palms, old knuckles broken
and stiff. This thumb can't flex
without snapping, bone on bone,
a clicker for Halloween. So this
is how we hold autumn in our hands.

Held wide, the fingers tremble, the fist
I pitched with, that held the stick
in Air Force jets, that slipped the ring
on my wife's finger, fists that held
three babies up to the world as if to beg
Be good, be careful with these kids.

THE MIDAS TOUCH IN TEXAS

I never needed much, a Midas touch,
a mile-wide ranch of Angus, a sky of geese
and rain clouds, a lovely woman who nibbles my ear
and then says *Please, hubby, love me.*
I've flown to Saigon and back, shot thousands of geese
on the flyway with cameras and prayed for rain,

hardscrabble dirt like rocks. We sank all we own
in babies, gave them their names and blessed them
as each left home. They gave back grandbabies we adore,
who gave us names, *Mamaw* and *Pop.* Nights,
we rock on the back porch, watching stars.
I'm stunned that a woman can be this lovely

at sixty. I thought old women and men
were only old. I see her eyes, the shadows
of her face, thin flecks of silver in her hair.
It hasn't rained in months, but I'm healed
wholly by her touch, amazed each time
she lifts my gnarled, stiff knuckles to her lips.

Marriage

The neighbors' dogs have howled at the last
siren and gone back to sleep.

The lights of the park switched off at midnight,
a dark garden of swings and fountains.

I hear jet-roar
far away like a waterfall.

This late at night she returns
with slow breaths, bearing vines

of the darkest grapes,
pomegranates which open soft as lips.

She knows my eyes are open
and kisses them shut so I can see.

Her fingers know the dark
corners of my mind,

her mouth repeats the mysteries,
her flesh becomes flesh.

Animals trot by outside our window
for the blessing of names.

WITCHING

The way to bring water gushing
out of stone is a secret a few old men
and women know—Moses, my Uncle Murphy
and others born to it, a priesthood
of dowsers witching water wells

with sticks. If a sycamore tree
led Zaccheus to living water,
Uncle Murphy claimed, it's sycamore for me.
I heard he brought in six wells
out of seven, one short

of perfect. False witches and prophets
rob the poor and turn young men
to scoffers. Men in their middle years
aren't sure: they wake at three or four,
crawl out of bed depressed

and doze in their easy chairs for hours,
counting the times a simple blood-pump
beats before it bursts. But wives
who've felt children come from nothing,
and children eager to believe

all things confess their faith
in witches. They believe at night,
almost asleep, release themselves
less consciously than prayer to dreams
all through the night.

AND HER FANS

Enter rare mud, real dirt, the lady
boys my age entered on tiptoes to ogle.
She swayed, dressed in white pasties
and feathers, the only wholly

naked thing we knew. State Fair barkers
let us in for a dollar bill
and a wink, slinking inside,
sitting on the edge of chairs

by men old enough to be our daddies.
This was the body we came for,
flesh worth slopping hogs for all year long,
worth all those winter hours milking cows

for entry fees. Now let it begin,
we whistled, rubbing our eyes all over her
on stage, our only sober work all day,
drunk on the dung of swine barns

ripe in the heat of October.
Never mind the tune, the scratch
of a warped record trying to turn
with every bump and grind of our lady.

She was our hearts' burden and desire,
to hold her feathers forever, groaning,
so close to pink fingernails
we could taste them.

HONKY-TONK BLUES

Shoving another quarter home to make
jukebox stars keep singing at night
in Texas, I think of Uncle Bubba
chopping wood, heaving his bad back
to it, in town again for a weekend.

Chips flew from his ax
like high notes. Puffing, he hummed
old country tunes that kept him fed
and human, half the honky-tonk clubs
in Texas more like his home

than Lubbock. Aunt Myrtie lived alone
five months out of six, pedaling
a Singer sewing machine to stay
faithful, trying to spin gold
from cotton threads and telegrams

he wired her twice a week. Whatever
she sewed sold fast at auction
in the mall and the county fair.
Now Bubba lives alone in a trailer park
in Austin, bait for tornadoes,

his stove a butane heater he seldom
lights. He sits outside as late
as his neighbors let him, strumming,
humming old songs like a scab
he keeps picking at over and over,

no new tunes ever right
for ballads about a cruel
good-hearted woman who let down
her spun silk rope one night
and slid out of his arms forever.

ALL THAT ACHES AND BLESSES

All that aches and blesses lives in the skin,
the thinnest organ, that turtle shell we scrub
and rub the wrong way daily like brass lamps
no genies rise from to save our bones
and ashes. We wade uncovered into guilt like ice
and curse the towels that leave the same thick
hide as always. We envy snakes that shed
their skins, chameleons that translate
themselves in colorful languages.
More than the heart, we give ourselves away
in skin, the blessing over all we are.
We feel the deepest loss of fathers
not in our bones, but skin they'll never touch.

THE MIDDLE YEARS

These are the nights we dreamed of,
snow drifting over a cabin roof
in the mountains, enough stacked wood
and meat to last a week, alone at last

in a rented A-frame, isolated,
without power, high in the San Juan.
Our children are safe as they'll ever be
seeking their fortune in cities,

our desk and calendar clear, our debts
paid until summer. The smoke of piñon
seeps back inside under almost invisible
cracks, the better to smell it. All day

we take turns holding hands and counting
the years we never believed we'd make it—
the hours of skinned knees and pleading,
diapers and teenage rage and fever

in the middle of the night, and parents
dying, and Saigon, the endless guilt
of surviving. Nights, we lie touching
for hours and listen, the silent woods

so close we can hear owls diving.
These woods are not our woods,
though we hold a key to dead pine planks
laid side by side, shiplap like a dream

that lasts, a double bed that fits us
after all these years, a blunt
front-feeding stove that gives back
temporary heat for all the logs we own.

TROUT FISHING IN THE ROCKIES

Near Creede where the Rio Grande runs clear
we backpack creels downstream, a flick,
flick to get the tight line flexing.

At first the pools back of boulders
for practice, sometimes a perfect cast
and strike as if winter never happened.

Crouched, we point at this pool,
that cutbank under the moss,
pretending trout can't see us.

Knowing trout are corrupt with hunger,
we offer flies like bribes.
Flicking our wrists out over stones

we reel in cutthroats and browns
from swift water as if nothing
but trout could save us.

BULLS AT SUNDOWN

Like a foreign god, the old herd bull
hauls himself uphill, rump and horns
see-sawing side to side. He's all alone
this close to darkness, bells of all cows

muffled by the barn, sweet odor
of fresh milk lazy from the stalls.
Calves waul and canter to the troughs,
shoving each other off and stumbling,

all of this having all and nothing to do
with him. Always in his corral of steel bars
a trough of grain is set, and so he comes
slowly between a ball of orange fire

in the west and dark rain-clouds,
time enough for standing still
and eating, swishing his tail
at horse flies always out of reach,

sun going down, an ache in his bones
like winter winds too soon,
the chaff tasteless and thin
like dry snow sticking to his lips.

STORIES WE SEEM TO REMEMBER

My father fished the Ouachita swamps
in winter, a sheet of ice so thin
even cast bait broke it,
squirrels sleeping overhead,
thousands of ducks at rest
after the Canadian flyway.

He was ten, able to go anywhere
alone, having no mother,
a father who turned corn liquor
out by the barrel, gone half the time
running his corn to market.

My father cooked his own stringer of fish,
slept by the warmth of the still
hidden by cypress, his arms
covered with chiggers and mosquito bites,
his boots the boots of his father
stuffed with bags of fish scales.
The first moccasin struck only a boot,
a fish-boy his uncles called Boots.

The next one gashed his heel
when he swam naked with my mother
the year of my birth,
the night the river bled
from my father's knife slash
in a swamp he'd gone back to visit,
no place I've seen but seem to remember,
and a tail lashing through water,
thrashing a current of blood.

NIGHT SHUTTLE

We'd leave after dark, windows down
to catch the first cool breeze all day.
Three to a seat, we squeezed
for elbow room, for pillows
and canteens and bags of snacks.

Before Daddy could shift the Ford
to high, Grandma raised her snuff can
to her lips, spittooing the brown
sweet stink. Hands on his knees,
leg and wide elbow gouging me,

Grandpa told us again how wagons
bounced when he was a boy,
no deep-pile cushions to sit on,
no sirree. Restless, without light
to read our stack of comics by,

my sister and I sneaked punches
at each other behind Grandpa's neck,
even though we knew the first
who hit him would get spanked.
For years we shuttled to Arkansas

by night in that black car
to bury Ozark relatives I never knew,
grandparents falling asleep,
our mother silent by the window,
staring at dark plains speeding past.

cicadas

Summer nights we ran for miles
around and around the only willow
in town, the long sheaves lashing our
vision dizzy, like crepe paper doorways
on Halloween, cicadas suddenly
clattering down on us, bursting
from thousands of willow limbs
like bats, like blind bats bumping
the leaves, banging their horn heads
against our faces, cicadas screaming
like klaxons, all of us screaming
and running faster
and faster from death.

All summer we entered the dark
limbs of that willow like a haunted
house filled with ghosts.
By winter, on branches like reeds,
we found them exposed, only
blunt shells split down the back.
We read them in silence as tokens,
as evidence of things not seen,
the thin shells clinging,
riding the whip of the wind
like sheets left behind by ghosts,
like hope gone underground
that would rise someday in new bodies
and haunt us the rest of our lives.

NIGHT OF THE SCORPION

Night of the scorpion, night of ice packs
and ankle swelling, my father tumbling stones
of a chimney fallen to rubble years ago,
fierce to kill whatever stung me.

In fever I rolled and tossed, saw his shadow
high in the willows, cast by the car lights,
broad back and head like a stinger
lunging from side to side, stones crashing
like thunder, like ninepins in the mountains.

All night I crawled through fire and forest,
gnashing my teeth, slicing my knees
on brimstones hissing and scuttling away.
Steam rising from fissures, screened demons
writhing and reaching for me. All night,
spiders died, mice died in their nests,
rocks burst and scattered like wind.

All day the next day my father slept,
unable to save me, his fingers raw
to the bone, my whole foot cold, swollen,
but a foot I could stand on
down on the same rubbled earth.

HIT and RUN

She is loosening my tie
with the slowest hands, fingers
that fan out through my hair.
I try opening my eyes,
but thumbs warm as lips
glide over them.
The siren coming through snow
is for me alone.
My knuckles are bleeding,
freezing to bricks.
The ambulance arrives softly,
blue light beaming, beaming.
This lady leans down as if
listening for my heart,
her breasts familiar as sleep.
I lie still in her arms
this enchanted evening in snow
I feel myself becoming.
When they lead her away
I try to hold on,
but they are lifting
my feet and shoulders
to a bed too narrow
for anyone but me.

LIVING IN NEXT-YEAR COUNTRY

We feed hardscrabble sand
green manure from a dairy. Seeds
we sprinkle like silver iodide
dry up and blow away. Nights, after hoeing
stalks trying to survive another drought,

we collapse, sipping homemade beer
from depression glass. We add and multiply
by lamplight, as if paper calves
could turn to cows. We should give up
on schemes to make this prairie dust

grow hooves. My father said Texas is
next-year country—next year it may rain,
next year we'll make two cotton bales to an acre
and buy a bull. We'd rather starve
than move away from land so flat it's ours.

The only asphalt road goes straight
a mile away. Even our dogs are farmers.
They drag home bones they find on other farms,
gnaw them dry and plant them. Unless it rains,
we'll never raise alfalfa for one calf.

Cow bones buried in the field may grow a herd
before we can. We sit outside at noon
under our only oak and watch hawks stalking snakes.
Wheeling, rising on thermals, they search for hours,
gliding in a sky so blank they stare.

THE Farm at Auction

It's gone, let garbled voices
auctioneer no more. The one bold gavel
gags us: *sold*. Don't give them tears,

it's over. Strange men in denim,
dealers, bidders from out of county
feel of my plows and heifers

like men reaching under my own wife's
dress, neighbors looking on,
my children standing by themselves

and staring. One grown farmer
could raise all the cotton
dirt could grow, if the bank

would let him, if foreign markets
stayed the same, if diesel didn't turn
to gold. Something in the sky

turned its back on us overnight,
something we've cursed but worked with
all these years—the threat of hail,

too little rain before harvest,
the reasonable gamble of sweat
in all seasons. How many times

do they sell all you own
to high bidders? Eighty dollars
to take that ditcher off my hands,

thank you for nothing. I paid
a thousand new and the paint's
not scratched, the blade is silver

from clay I broke it through.
I should be used to this by now,
plowing flat fields for nothing

I can keep. Come on, lift up your end
of this oak hope chest and heave it
aboard. There's room in the pickup

for this and more, but not for tears.
Lift up your city head
and look around: it's gone.

CROSSING THE ROAD

What's a boy to do, both shoes caught in the tar,
the road past our house turning to street,
and me, a chicken trying to reach the other side.
Men burly as uncles swore and shook their shovels,

laughing. My mother waited on the porch,
drying her hands in her apron. My big sister teased,
her gawky girlfriends howled, and someone screamed
Tar baby! I swear I tugged, cursing the only words

I had learned, squashed down in July asphalt
like a bug, like Captain Marvel in the comics
turned into a tree, unable to budge. And of all days,
on my birthday. Carl would see me soon, and Mary Jane,

all kids I knew pointing on the curb and dancing.
Like God roaring up on his motorcycle, my brother
dismounted and stared. Tucking a Camel in his lips,
he lit and flipped the match away, came strolling down,

fists doubled, snorting smoke, not smiling.
Massive, towering above me, he jerked me up
without my shoes and hauled me like a sack of oats
back to the grass, his own boots ruined.

I remember him that way, not the box of belongings
they brought from Okinawa, not the flag Mother hung
in the window for all cars to see speeding past
the four-lane street, pounding my sneakers down.

BAPTIZING THE DOG AT NINE

I heard puppies have no souls,
but I loved that mongrel with a bulldog mom.
Behind the barn, I preached that dog's head down
until he dozed. His stubby tail said *Yes, I believe
whatever you say*. Crows in the arbor cawed like scoffers.

I staggered with thirty grunting pounds, shoved him
to the stock tank and huffing said the words
and dumped him. He splashed and came up paddling,
head up and wholly dunked, shock of pond scum
in his eyes. The startled crows swirled off,

a flutter of black hosannahs. I thought he'd rise
and talk like Balaam's donkey, but he thrashed
as if drowning. Slick-haired, he never barked.
I had to drag him out, his glazed eyes hopeless,
fat crows in the arbor cawing.

AUNT LINDA AND THE PINK BIKINI

Her tongue was spice and lightning
even at nineteen. She caught her husband
playing doctor with a nurse and cursed him,
calling all doctors frauds. She kept his name

for herself, the cars and house for their children.
She sold most stocks for a wardrobe. In time,
Cadillacs came by, Mercedes, pickups with gun racks—
I couldn't count the cowboy boots that strutted

to her door. Men liked her summer laugh,
pink thongs and terry cloth. I remember Aunt Linda
in bikinis at picnics, divorced in-law, but family.
I was bold with mustard for her burgers,

the perfect nephew. Linda always had a sticky kiss
for me, and whispered six-packs of advice—*Shave close
and take no prisoners*. She clipped me on the chin
and left sweet lipstick on my cheek. One year,

I listened hard and heard Aunt Linda whisper vows
in a veil Uncle Cal lifted—she made me call
the tall cowboy that—and he kissed her
glistening lips, and all the family sighed.

ADOPTION

We took them in our arms, those washed,
donated blankets and week-old babies,
bare facts scratched on tablet paper—
their foster parents' chronicles
of formula and colic, their bottles
and pajamas, their oddly temporary names.

Three babies in different years, the lightest loads
we'd ever hold. That was the Sixties
before I went to Vietnam and back,
branded vicious, a baby killer. Such hope
never happened again, the whole world's peace
at risk. Those wise caseworkers knew about loss,

half trauma nurses, half Santa Claus.
Joyful, we took the babies they gave,
miraculous heartbreak, each almost weightless,
shockingly small, almost too delicate to take
from the arms of a woman who knew how to bring
and let go. I can still feel the cling

of fingers wrapped around mine,
the charm of tiny eyes squeezed tight.
We held each baby in the neon gaze
of the state's agency, helpless, tall,
heart-pounding strangers these babies came to—
voices they'd never heard, might never

have picked—big-fisted, dazed,
throat-choked and humming lullabies,
blur-eyed, not caring who might see.
We were only a couple holding a baby
giddy and trembling with questions, and clumsy,
but parents, and our baby was crying.

WHAT OLD PILOTS SAY

Play with it, say it out loud when you're alone,
if that will help. Gnaw horror like a bone,
suck blood and marrow out. Reach behind your face
and turn it off, like lights-out on the base.
Someone will die today, tonight. Rockets fall,
some posts get overrun. That's what the guards
and body bags are for. You can't fly without sleep.
Tell your first sergeant, *Wake me*
if they break through the lines. Otherwise
let it lie. Take it one flight at a time.

Home won't come by holding your balls
and breath too tightly in your fist. Jog,
play handball, cut back on booze and easy lays
after you're back. Look both ways
in Asian skies, swivel your crash-helmet head.
When your wingman spots a missile, break
any way he says. One flight at a time.
Go back to the world, your only wife,
breed lots of kids and tell your lies.
Or not. Some of us have to die.

ROCKET ATTACK

Crack like a screen door slammed
and cannon fire. After that first explosion,
silence, then fallout that clattered down.
I heard shouts and sirens and saw men run,

the roar of choppers and gunfire at dawn,
the rumble of bombs. I remember the weird
thrill of falling hard as they taught,
someone throwing up next door in fear.

I remember waking later, stunned that I slept
after that. I followed echoes in my skull
to the shattered hootch, airmen dead
in a crater fifty feet east—their blood

splattered like motor oil. MPs stood guard,
and corpsmen sifted smoking dirt for bones
or flesh. I remember breakfast was lard
and runny eggs with ketchup and burned toast

butter-soaked, and bacon fried soggy
in a tent reeking of greasy smoke and wood.
It seemed insane—*but the fragile body
was hungry, and it was good, it tasted good.*

WITH MERCY FOR ALL

She was a mystery of give and take,
laid open to strangers and neighbors in need,
no thought of lawsuits in those innocent days.
She took abuse from people she helped feed
in the Texas depression, who quarreled
and promised to pay her back, but frowned
and walked away when they saw her
after church. Our mother never doubted
evil was merely need in neighbors.
She carried fables with her to the grave,
although she saw her father pistol-whipped
for giving a man a ride in winter.
A thousand nights she sat with the aged,
the sick and the dying. At thirty-eight,
she ran bare-footed to save a child,
jerking him up from the screaming mother
and pumping the marble out. Then collapsed in the briars
coming back, had to be helped home by others.
My sister tweezered sixty stickers from her feet.
Mother moaned how thankful she missed them
going over, though dozens stuck to her feet
when she ran to that baby on adrenaline
and faith. She never fathomed how pluck happened
throughout her life, how fast it left her
lovely and flushed, trembling with a funeral fan
in her hand, a comely woman, mother, nurse,
who believed herself simple, submissive, afraid,
not knowing how able she was, how recklessly brave.

Halfway Between the Gulf and Mountains

We memorized each other's eyes before Saigon,
casting for bass after dark, hearing the splash
and battle in the shallows. Driving back, we watched hawks
glide over piñon and spruce and disappear.
I rode the brakes around steep switchbacks.

Centuries slid past the last wide turns.
We saw black granite cracked by juniper roots,
the bark sloughed off, stumps twisted by winds.
Woodcarvers rub for weeks to groove the grain
that smooth—rings around wounds

grown perfect, curves no lathe could turn.
So many years, and no more friends come back.
I've been to the wall and rubbed my fingers on their names,
faces in polished granite. Now, we watch the dawn
and let the sun sustain us halfway between the Gulf of Mexico

and mountains. Nothing on these flat plains is like the war,
except sometimes asleep. Good neighbors offer fruit
from gardens on rationed water. Even our dogs
feel at home. They raise wet muzzles to the moon
and howl at stars so far away they stare.

Traveling in Packs

A splash, and sharp teeth drag the wildebeest
down, off balance, thrashing in slippery mud,
jerked to the churning foam of its own blood feast,
into the rushing river swollen by the flood,

kicked by the hoofs of wild-eyed others leaping
and splashing, the beast still kicking for breath,
but feebly, nearly paralyzed by fear and the death grip,
one crocodile thrashing to snap its neck,

tail flip and fangs sunk deeply into the throat
going under, dragging it into the darkest water
this wildebeest ever crossed, legs limp, as if floating,
coughing its goat-like bark under water,

the hungry herd scrambling up to the plains,
traveling in packs in the food chain,
a thunder of splashing hoofs and groans
over the swirl of bodies already bloated,

the bubble eyes of beasts like unexpected guests
with scales and appetites and tails, slowly
nosing upstream, without hurry,
choosing which one, which one is next.

OLD PETS

Hawks in wide, hardscrabble skies track mice
in fields we say we own. We feed too many pets
our children raised by hand and abandoned.
Old bulls aren't worth the hay to save them,

but I don't throw away a glove because it's ugly.
Look at them, old goats and horses fat in the pasture.
That palomino's lame, the oldest mare on the plains,
drools when I rub her ear, can't hear unless I whisper,

leans on me like a post, slobbering oats from my glove,
swishing her tail. This abandoned barn was weeds,
the padlock missing. Thieves hauled good metal off,
nothing but someone's dream holding a roof over stalls,

the cows long slaughtered. Owls watched the plunder of doors
in silence. A man with children built this barn
to last, but not one stayed to carry on his herd.
We had to track them down to sign. And now the barn is ours,

and pastures fenced by barbed wires dangling from posts,
and most of those are broken. We might as well breed wolves
or trap for bounty snakes that kill our calves.
We could sell the rattlers' venom for research,

and wolves are bred for national parks in Montana
so why not here? Dawn, I shake my head at my schemes
and saddle up, time for rounding strays
and dumping hay to old pets bawling at the barn.

AUNT FANNY AND THE NEIGHBORS' NAGS

Her horses nibbled sugar, our palms barely wet.
The way mares grazed made *horse-face*
not a put-down, after all. *They ate polite*,
Aunt Fanny said, a long-boned widow from Paducah.

When Uncle Joe passed on, she bought a farm
and turned the stalks to pastures, built stalls
for doctors' and lawyers' horses and her own.
Fanny worked magic with ponies and depressed old nags,

trapped all their lives in town back lots. At first,
mares stood in the stalls heads down, stiff lipped
and wooden like Washington's false teeth.
Aunt Fanny talked to them all like daughters

awkward in training bras. Briskly she brushed
and curried, and led them around the pasture,
one at a time, then two, then a herd of old girls
clopping along, wild enough within months

to gallop without coming back sad to the barn
as if beaten or left alone too long. Even us
they let duck under their necks and stroke
and hold, hearing their hearts' deep bumps,

accepting sugar cubes we lifted to gray lips
nibbling, not nipping a finger, old muzzles
quivering, ripples of horse hairs
grazing our necks like fringe.

NIGHTS ON THE PORCH SWING

I see from my wife's dark eyes
we're not alone. Our stock tank
shimmers in moonlight. Whatever warns her

makes her squeeze my neck—a whiff of fear,
a riffle of feathers. Owls own the earth,
round eyes thrust downward. I've seen her

rescue five baby ducks a day, a night-light on
for ducks waddling spoiled in the washroom.
On the swing, I talk of hunger,

the natural curve of talons. *Hush*,
she warns me. Her body knows the rhythms
of the moon, expects owls most nights

and ignores them. Tonight, her fingers
strum the short hairs of my neck.
We hear a scream squeezed out by talons.

I shove the porch swing higher with my boots,
but her moccasins stop us,
dragging the swing off balance. *Hush*,

she says, her nails in my flesh.
She tugs my beard and squeezes,
her fingers stroking, stroking my neck.

WHATEVER THE WIND DELIVERS

This is the rage for order on the plains,
barbed wire cinched tight from post to post.
Acres of land each year go back to sand

and disappear. Nothing not tied down
stays home. Canadian geese fly over us
each fall, each spring, and never stay.

Our steers two times a year trudge up
board ramps to slatted walls of trucks
from the slaughterhouse. Even our children

rise up like owls and fly away. Nights,
you turn for me to hold you. We pretend
we go away by writing French love notes

in dust on the headboard. At dawn,
you smooth oiled cloths over all we wrote
the night before. By dusk, the film is back,

the earth we live on, the dust our fingers
string new fences on, holding each other
one more night with loving words.

Rattler

Coiled, it's crazy and hostile, without a lawyer,
tail rattling like dice in a plastic cup. *Mine*,
its tongue flicks out, guarding nothing but rocks
and cactus, its eyes squeezed tight

nursing a grudge, alone and wandering forty years
in the desert, the loss of gardens not its fault,
nobody had to gamble the family farm on its advice,
its diamonds squeezed in the fist of its muscle

bulged and stingy like a gut, nothing but a mouth
with fangs and a knotty large intestine,
devouring all it can swallow, all it can kill.
I told my grandsons never bend down by a woodpile,

never go barefoot in cactus, but their Frisbee
angled off from the yard, wobbled and rolled
in the weeds. I saw them and hobbled, calling,
almost too late to save them, snatched one in each arm

and leaped back, panting. We watched the old pretender
coil and sway like a magic rope and squirm away,
head weaving from side to side, as if nodding
from cactus to cactus, *Mine, mine*.

THE SUMMER OUR GRANDSONS TURNED TWELVE

When that old, fat black lab wobbled,
both of us stopped talking and watched him hobble
like a bull-beast nightmare staggering down the stairs.
Creaky, spoiled-rotten Dino plopped by our chairs,
blessing us both with sweet-sour apple breath
like some old monk's who knows all foibles

of the human heart, but rest assured, he loves us.
Five years after his brother died, sprayed by skunks,
battered by gout and fights with stray dogs,
he slept inside on winter nights, wheezing, our bodyguard
barking for sunshine. One black eye, scarred,
saw visions. Only the other, pearly blue, could focus.

Sleeping, he snored, kicking the floor like clubs.
How fast he aged, twelve years like months—a pup
when our twin grandsons kicked and stared at mobiles
hovering above their cribs, cooing and twisting
when they heard that happy, high-pitched yip,
the ball of fur we held for them to touch.

GRANDDADDY'S KNUCKLES

Cotton spun from his blades, and grain
taller than men. He taught me to plow,
his rows so straight I could follow.
I believed whatever he put in the earth

would grow. When he prayed for rain,
it rained. Now, his plows have no answers,
parked in the barn. Granddaddy's grip
is there on rods rough as his palms

which swung me up to his neck.
I rode his massive shoulders,
plowing thin fringes of his hair,
ducking under beams of his ceiling.

When he tipped his Stetson,
hawks dipped their wings good-bye,
gliding on thermals. I touched his scars,
his leather skin like bull hide.

I asked how he learned about snakes
and coyotes, the secrets of owls,
why all his hair turned white.
Now, when I swing my grandson up

to my shoulders, he strokes my knuckles,
my thinning hair. Holding his arms,
I feel him leaning, staring at my face,
amazed I could be so old.

Historical Markers

Our tires crunch down off the highway,
the sign like a miner's claim, *Here*,
Coronado's men crossed *here*, a gravel turnout
with a trash barrel. Wind whips past the car,
the fields so wide we're stranded, a barn

blurred in the shimmer, a mirage we swear
is water. In this heat, nothing lopes.
If coyotes sniff us, they blink and listen.
Nothing's here, not even cattle.
Coronado's horses were lost, following cactus

staked like markers across the plains.
I hear the clink of armor, the thin
curse, Spanish word for *God*.
Squinting west where we're headed,
I hear the clank of pans in their wagon,

the thunder of eight hundred hooves.
Soldiers slump in the saddles,
cursing the last buffalo wallow,
canteens already hot, following Coronado
sweaty in his high-peaked Spanish hat,

no gold, nothing between camps
but white bones scattered, a desert
unmapped where they might die without water,
nothing to mark their route, to pause
and lift forgotten names to God.

TURNING FIFTY

My wife sips tomato juice
in turbulence. In clouds, we sway and bump
with plastic glasses balanced in our fists.

Her hand flies high in a down draft,
falls hard to the tray, and wide-eyed
she laughs. Seat-belt signs flash on,

attendants down, strapped in. She glances out
at lightning. The plane slams hard,
a door pops open and luggage tumbles out.

Somewhere, a woman screams. The captain's voice
comes on, mellow as Muzak, *Folks, lean back
and enjoy the flight, and we'll have you in Dallas*

right on time. My wife shakes a wrist
to get the cold blood pumping. Her hand
is messy with a cracked plastic glass of ice.

I lean giddy to her eyes, my hand slick as hers,
my juice glass sloshing like champagne,
and lift it dripping to her lips.

GRANDFATHER'S MATCHED PALOMINOS

Here's the hack Grandfather bought in Austin,
saved by a tarp like an awning against dust,
the droppings of barn owls. A postman
and circuit rider before World War I,

he brought parcels and the gospel to cowboys
and squatters, married a rancher's daughter
and bought this buggy for their babies.
Mules could pull it, but later Grandfather hitched

matched palominos, the only vain things he owned.
No other horse or Model T could beat him to the hunt
or steepled church in town, the first shack on the plains
with bats. He gave up all he owned for war,

forty when he left for Flanders, captain's bars
he bargained for like Faust. I knew him old,
a humped man laughing at my hand stands
and wobbly somersaults. He applauded

and tossed me candy he kept like magic
inside his roll-top desk next to his rocking chair.
He never showed the scars, the pistols I wondered
if he brought back. He gave away his medals,

everything but Bibles and the ranch.
Mother's brothers sold the ranch and left her
with investments and what was still in the barn
after auction, a saddle with a broken horn,

assorted ropes and bridles, the branding irons
they didn't take, a framed tintype of two palominos,
the hack with a cracked leather whip
my mother claimed he never, ever used.

WHEN CHILDREN THINK YOU CAN DO ANYTHING

Living on hardscrabble, a man is less
than a wolf and knows it, carries a rifle
in season or not. Out here, killing's
always in season, time enough for scruples
sweating in bed with the windows raised.

I hear my kids kicking their sheets.
Like good kids, they blame the heat.
I feel my wife's heat inches away.
They sleep with only me to protect them,
nothing outside I haven't tracked for years,

bobcats and wolves, rattlers that coil
under our trailer like tribal gods.
I'm paid to patch fences around a range
nothing but goats and cows could graze.
I keep the stock tanks full, the buzzards hoping.

When cows stray down arroyos, the wolves
are sure to follow, circling a calf too weak
to waddle. If I can drop one wolf by moonlight,
the others tuck-tail and run. If I'm late,
next morning I drive the cow out

wide eyed and frothing, her full bag swaying,
mesquite and cactus wedging us apart. That night,
I splash my face a long time at the pump
and comb my hair and shave, roll down my sleeves
and go inside as if nothing's happened.

CATTLE IN RAIN

No cow knows what to do in rain.
Grackles dive for the trees
and chickens flap for the barn,
squeezing their wings and waddling.

Caught in the fields, cows
shove their muzzles down
and graze. Something in the sky
is falling. Their round eyes glaze,

and everywhere they stare
is green. They never blink,
they drop their dished heads
down and grind off all grass

they can reach. They believe
when it is time to lie down
in the pasture, they will go on
chewing this green haze forever.

FEEDING THE WINTER CATTLE

We lifted bales and dropped them heavy
from the wagon. Hay burst like melons,
even on a cushion of snow. Plodding,

a bossy cow took charge of each split bale,
head down, her long horns hooking air,
her purple tongue sucking the bale like a melon.

Dumbly, the others followed, bobbing their heavy heads.
Stark sunshine made me squint, watching a hawk.
The dogs weaved behind the wagon, panting,

sniffing for tracks, wetting the wagon
when it stopped. The mules didn't care,
stubborn as if asleep in their harness.

Grandpa coaxed, "Please, sir, Big Ed.
Once more for daddy, Lou," tapping black reins
like a love pat. And bump, we'd lurch again,

my little brother and I grabbing for balance
on floor boards slick with straw,
stabbing our gloves into another bale

and lifting, heaving it over like ballast
between the dogs, like another Christmas visit
dropping away forever.

FATHER'S REVOLVER

I carried it cold, with pearl handles.
Behind the outhouse, I spun the gun like a cowboy.
Rabbits die because their world is full of rattlers.
They run from boys with their fathers' revolvers,
but not far. I twirled that silver pistol

until I seldom dropped it, spinning it over and over
and plop, into the holster—the fastest gun in Texas.
I thought now it begins, the endless cycle
of gunfighters. I dreamed my aim could save me,
the heavy Colt not cocked but loaded. I believed

the secret was simply to draw, certain I could drop
actors in black hats wide as barns. Spitting
on weeds, I tossed a fruit jar up and pointed,
bang! I said, and it exploded. Tilting the pistol,
I blew as if the cold barrel smoked,

as if I'd shot. Lifting it up, I studied
the snub tips of bullets like secrets of girls
covered by silk or cotton. I rolled
the cylinder and watched each bullet loaded.
I knew my father would hear, but I could say

backfires of cars on the dirt road, not thinking
there'd be no plumes of dust for miles. I groped
both thumbs to cock it, waving it like a wand
over the pasture, coaxing rabbits to hop boldly
in the open, daring rattlesnakes to coil.

THE ONE THAT GOT AWAY

We took turns eating ammonia dirt,
Billy Ray and me and big Joe Bubba,
bucked off in the corral, dying to tame
the tiger springing under us with hooves,
broad muscles bulging the saddle loose.

That horse would make a champion palomino,
tamed, a showboat stallion, prancer in parades.
First one to ride could have him,
old Uncle Oscar swore, his bad back stiff,
or he'd have broken it himself.

How many times did Slick buck us,
how many kicks to our heads,
just missing? After split lips
and sunburns, we turned him loose,
the deal we made with Uncle Oscar. Cursing,

loving that stud like no other, we swore
we'd find him again when we were older,
him and his harem of mares. After we finally
flicked off the reins, after Joe Bubba
let down the gate, Billy Ray coaxed

that palomino until it bolted away
out of the dust and horse dung,
free over the wide dry prairie,
four hooves in the air forever,
his mane like flames of gold.

UNCLE ROLLIE AND THE LAWS OF WATER

The windmill pumps an old, slow action up and down,
like making prairie love for water. Fat cattle
worshipped a trough Rollie kept full on flat plains
made for coyotes. He shared with farmers getting started,
let them open and close his gates to haul sloshing barrels
in wagons, helped dozens dig their own sweet water wells.
He taught me to draw, that perfect slap of leather,

the bang and wavering whine across a mile of pasture.
I needed what only he could offer, a horse to ride,
a thousand acres of rabbits, tales of range wars
and buffalo. But I was ten and he was sixty,
old as heroes in the Bible, childless like Abraham,
Aunt Mary dead before my older brother was born.
When Rollie died, steers wandered these acres

like a desert, getting fat for an absentee landlord
who must be dead. The last barbed wires are down,
the whine of buzz saws building imported lumber,
his pasture sold as tracts for houses. This windmill
is the last he dug, the stock tank shot by rifles,
the water trickling through a rusted pipe, faithful
after all these years, the dry, split blades still turning.

WILDCATTING

In the cramped cab of a pickup, we bump down
caliche canyons between mesquite and cactus,
following hunch and arroyos more than maps.

Whatever covers oil is old and barren,
dry riverbeds, patches of bone-white alkali,
outcroppings of granite,

a billion barrels ours for the drilling.
Nothing is there until we find it.
We believe in steel bits and stone

and twist our wrenches tight,
drunk on the constant spinning, each twist
of the bit like love, trying it over and over.

THE NIGHT OF RATTLESNAKE CHILI

Only the lure of a rattler kept us
jerking dry tumbleweeds back
from the bunkhouse. Already, cook had
chili boiling, peppers and beef
convincing us all we were starving.

Cursing, throwing empty bean cans
at our horses, cook swore he'd douse
the fire and dump our dinner to the mules
unless we brought him a long dry tail
of a rattler. I had heard of cooks

crazy enough to grind rattles
like chili powder, a secret poison
to make a pot boil darker than whiskey.
Kicking and calling each other names,
we scoured the range for an hour,

a ranch so cursed with snakes
jackrabbits weren't safe while mating.
At last, I grabbed one by the tail,
the writhing muscle trying to escape
down a burrow, and Billy Ray shot it.

Cook cut off the tail and grinned,
held up the ticking rattle, then
crushed and ground it in his hands.
Hulls floated down into red steam,
and simmered. That night, we ate

thick chili redder than fire
and griped about the dust and hulls,
but begged for seconds. Even our beer
was cold and sweeter than most
and steel spoons melted in our mouths.

DRIVING HOME TO THE PLAINS

Now it begins, the endless golds
and blues, no forests,
no mountains anywhere.
Sunshine sixteen hours a day,

nothing to shade us, not even
an eclipse. Parched lips seek each other
for escape, the cracked bruising
making blood. Fields this flat

sprawl like the moon,
like Mars. Nothing about the place
resembles home. On land this flat
no wonder people pray, left out all night

like babies that fell off wagons
heading west, weeping all night
for bottles, blankets, nothing ever more
but sky, ten million stars.

OLD MEN FISHING AT BROWNWOOD

Spitting tobacco juice on hooks,
we skewer silver minnows that writhe
in the light of the moon, lining our boat
with bass fighting for all the line

they're worth. These are the shallows,
the home of the moccasins, deep mud
of the turtles. Our flat boat wallows,
bumps over stumps, and stalls. Slowly,

slapping mosquitoes, we pole it off
and glide in moonlight between branches
like scarecrows. What we desire
winnows the dark under logs

flooded for years, in tunnels of reeds,
deep pools in the shallows. We believe
we will know what we need when we find it,
though it may take nights on still water,

for we are too old to turn back, to settle
for perch in the daylight, willing to risk
pneumonia or stroke, the hiss of fangs
nearby on a shimmer of water.

NIGHT MISSIONS

Tonight will be like any other night.
At two or three the phone will ring
soon as I've drawn the first good hand.
I'll spread the cards face up,
knowing solitaire won't peek. Pecos,
Abilene, it could be anywhere
south of Denver, someone badly burned,
skull crushed like a hard-boiled egg,
needing a surgeon in the Southwest
who could put him together again.

I fire up number one, then two, propellers
spinning so smooth the Cessna shudders
until I release the brakes. I taxi out,
in the red glow of the cockpit
I run the checklist, flip on collision lights
and find all gauges in the green.
I hit the runway, fire-wall both throttles
and line up on the roll.
Banking, I'll clip the moonlight,
blue wings climbing somebody's dreams,
tuned blades humming like mercy.

sandstorms

How many nights can we take it,
the constant blither of wind,
the splatting of sand

on the windows? We would pray
for rain, even floods, here
where nothing comes of all our

tossing and turning, trying
to sleep, but dust in the morning
to whisk away with oilcloths.

Nothing can keep it out,
not locks, not wet towels
plastered to the cracks. Dust

floats through every room.
Even our feet as we tiptoe
tap up a plume,

a soft tattoo of dust that follows
everywhere, an echo of outside
weather. We wash sheets

twice a week and slip between
clean percale already grainy,
our bodies rubbing away to dust.

THE BARN ON THE FARM WE'RE BUYING

We slide the barn door wide and cough. Dust swarms,
the half-buried droppings of horses and owls
like feather dusters uncleaned for decades.
The rattle of rollers echoes in the barn,
abandoned to straw never changed. Hames of horses

creak when we lift them. Our flashlights
sweep past empty stalls. Dust floats
from every beam, embalming all but us.
Not even a barn owl stares, digesting
last night's mice. We tap the walls,

the sturdy posts. Why do we talk hardly above
a whisper, when no one's close enough to hear
and we hold the deed? Did he care
strangers would buy his barn
when he and his horses were gone?

Where are the rotten planks
we'd counted on, the cracked rafters,
the sagging roof? How can we tear down walls
he built to last? Where are the layers
of gauze cobwebs we thought would serve

as kindling? On these dry plains,
can't even spiders live? Nothing in the barn
seems old but leather, and dust
we're growing used to, our other odor,
the earth we're beginning to call home.

GOAT RANCHING

I could let go and live with the goats
that forage our mesquite and cactus,
browsing on grass, salt blocks

and cardboard boxes that tumble up,
and saunter to the tank to drink.
They've never killed a kid by kindness

or neglect, never had to put their kids'
old dogs to sleep, friends
that drool and quiver and stumble

hobbling to our hands. I've never
seen a goat afraid of trouble. Horny,
they strip the bark off cedar posts

and stand for hours in moonlight,
whetting their horns like sabers
on barbed wires.

LOSING a BOAT on THE Brazos

Downriver rocks were rapids. Believe me,
even fish have ears. Sweating, we coasted
too far out on a river we've fished
for forty years. I swear it's never
been this low, but two old cousins
can't keep the Brazos full forever.

Sharp rocks are death to aluminum boats
harder to split than wood. We're safe,
spitting out mud and minnows, but alive
after months of drought and a soaking.
Bury the boat and forget it.
We could have drowned any wet year

under tons of the Brazos flooding
downhill to the dam. We could be food
for alligator gar and catfish.
That rip is wider than the lies
we'll tell for months, the size of bass
that got away, the granddaddy cat

we finally caught that flipped
and disappeared through the hole
of the boat, going down. Let's sit
on the bank and laugh at why we let
eight hundred dollars of rods and tackle
sink and saved a shell worth less

than beer cans we crush for salvage
every day, two old fools splashing ashore,
dragging a gashed boat out
as if dry land could save it,
like old bones mired in mud we've proved
can rise and walk again.

For Friends Missing in Action

Often I've caught a glint of silver,
fliers trusting their dials and wing tips.

Odd, walking flat sand after years in a cockpit,
caught between the earth and angels. How many loops

and barrel rolls, thrusting from earth
inverted, how many dives and pull-outs,

straining to stop blood rushing from my skull.
I see young pilots on TV, faces lined

from their masks, cropped hair and ancient eyes,
the stance of tigers. I remember Millard

and Roy Carnes shot down in jungle,
Bob Ross and Jones, and Billy Ray Moegle,

the squadron clown, dragged through Hanoi,
still missing—fellows on fire with laughter,

God on our side through any skies we dared,
the future paved with runways leading home.

praise

It's four, Montana cabin cold.
I lift a blanket past her arms
and slip outside with coffee,
valley so still I hear the Amtrak
to Seattle miles away. No breeze
or stars, the deck so cold

steam rises like a rope trick
from the cup. The moon plays poker
with a deck of clouds, and folds.
Last week, a pack of wolves downwind
raised muzzles to the moon and howled,
prowlers of mountains back in Montana.

Praise dark before the dawn.
Praise God who made the dawn
and water tumbling down from snow,
the tap I'll turn today. Praise God
for sleep, for grizzlies
wild in the mountains, and massive.

For breath that puffs away,
for this dark day, the sun
we're spinning around, the moon
I believe is out there past the clouds.
For my wife's closed eyes
I need to open once more, soon.

THAT CHILD ABANDONED ON THE PORCH

In that child in tonight's newscast
I see our son, wandering Montana.
With luck, he'll find what he's missing,
hunting for gold or answers. What odds
brought him to us, a million to one,
ten million? The darkest hair, his eyes

squeezed tight in the agency's bright lights.
That nurse must have swaddled babies
a thousand times, but to us she was an angel
and we mere shepherds in from the cold.
There, near the gold-domed Denver capital, star
on a highway map, there where they gathered taxes

in mountains, there we had come with nothing
but wads of paper telling us the birth hour,
not even the baby's weight, only that he
was the one, all of our luck in one boy,
and when we held him, he was,
he was the child in our arms.

Praying for Rain on the Plains

If it comes,
let tractors stall hub-deep.
Pull off your boots and walk without socks,
squeeze globs of what you are. Feel mud like Vaseline,
the crushed and processed ferns and dinosaurs.
In a million years we'll ooze from vaults
and metal caskets, back in the mud where we belong.
Even West Texas dirt grows beans and cotton,
peppers that make us weep. Let rain come
by the bucket, let prices soar after floods,
let it hail. Pastors throughout the Plains have prayed.
Farmers who sulk at home and tinker with plows
while their wives drive pickups to church,
even burned, skin-cancer atheists
stare at flat horizons without a cloud
and blink.

TORNADO CHASING

At night the cell phone crackles
and I back out. Hail pounds the pickup.
I drive for hours under blurred lightning
on highways. Now I can find it

if it's here. In twenty years I've seen
a thousand twisters. Most nights, I'm the fool
they think I am, risking my life
for nothing. But they listen like prayer

for my eyewitness news, and they believe.
Bouncing down dirt roads, I call
Tornado sighted and chase the devil's
tongue until the road dead-ends

or the thunder dies. They know the force
I follow, the vacuum of black funnels
in flashes. They gasp like me
and breathe the name of God.

WRESTLING WITH ANGELS

All night, hip out of joint,
he holds the stranger's arms,
throws him twice but can't pin him
to the earth: shoulder blades

flex like wings and spring him loose.
The man is not even breathing hard.
Jacob knows. Hobbling,
he plants his good heel for leverage.

Their footprints in the dirt
scrape out the six points of a star. Lunging,
he clutches the arms and they spiral
like dancers. Jacob shuts his eyes tight,

tight, and holds on. At dawn
the blessing comes: watch him,
breathless, pull on his new name
Israel like a robe.

THE War In Bosnia

Under darkness of stars our son flies
over Bosnia, keeping watch over snow,
Apache gunships will be out tonight.

The moon on foreign snowfields highlights
bodies running under trees, friend or foe.
Under darkness of stars our son flies

with star scope and rockets and wide eyes
over war zones bitter enemies know.
Apache gunships will be out tonight.

What keeps a nation armed and justifies
air power is such a killing field—we know,
but under darkness of stars our son flies.

In boots and parka, someone watches the skies
and owns disposable Stingers, and is cold.
Apache gunships will be out tonight.

I conjure God to stop him, warp his sights.
I stare with the prayer all fathers know.
Under darkness of stars our son flies.
Apache gunships will be out tonight.

BARGAINING WITH GOD

Walt McDonald's granddaughter Jennifer, who inspired this poem,
passed from this life on August 29, 2004

I switch from praying hands to fists.
It's the itch of a trigger finger
without a gun, digging out from rubble
at the tower of Babel, grunting,
yearning to speak in tongues.

I'm long past rage, most days,
bearing the DNA of Cain
even at this age. I don't dread the Bomb
or tornadoes. Falling asleep, I beg Take me
instead of my darlings. Take the ranch

and bank account, the mountain cabin,
but save our granddaughter now.
Let me be Job in rags, Jeremiah
in tears, but heal this little child now.
I prophesy how many test tubes it takes,

how many angels dancing on a highway
could stop a drunk from swerving
into the doctor who might find
a cure—if not today, tomorrow,
good God, soon.

WITH MY SON'S BOW AT DUSK

I call and hear a thistle flick the house.
Another weed I missed, too busy to take time.
My son comes running with his bow,

empty quiver flouncing on his back.
Whatever he shot in the arbor he missed,
maybe pears too green to pick. The full moon

bulges, and next day's lessons wait.
Tomorrow we'll hunt the arrows,
and I'll say again don't shoot

unless he can follow the feathers
and find them. Tousle-haired and eight,
he hands me the bow and runs,

and the backdoor slams. I almost call,
but I'm eight again myself, and lift the bow
and aim, pretending, string taut

and tingling in my tips, the arbor dark,
one shadow darker and gobbling,
one last fat turkey I can't miss.

DRIVING AT NIGHT across Texas

Her arms held all the songs I longed for,
and four tires took me there.
I was a pilot at a base on the border,
more time on the highway than flying,
driving at night across Texas,

humming all the old songs.
But we keep losing our heroes,
grandparents and singers, friends
missing in action. Car wrecks take them away,
or drugs, planes that crash in mountains

or winter fields, or plain old death.
I think of Glenn Miller in World War Two,
Patsy Cline and Billie Holiday, and a boy
from my hometown named Buddy Holly.
Seven grandchildren after a war,

Vietnam is always a fact—*there it is*,
even in dreams. Some go on
in hospital beds or wheelchairs,
some so boldly brave I'm stunned.
I rock with my wife under stars

on the lawn swing, stroking the same hair
dark as it was those nights in Austin
when the world seemed like a bandstand
and we had coins enough forever,
the jukebox full of songs.

THE Year BIOLOGY MaDe Sense

When brunette Trudy moved to town,
we boys in fourth grade saw
what biology was for. We'd heard,

but sullen girls were nothing to us
but skinny kids who rolled their eyes
and made good grades. They whispered a lot

and wept and never played our games.
But sleepy-eyed Trudy came in April,
near the end of school, and all she taught

we learned. To watch her cross the room
was college. Trudy was curves and honey,
the show-and-tell for well-thumbed magazines

big brothers hid, and cars we found
abandoned at the park. Then, theology
and math made sense, the parables

of puppy love and Oz. When Trudy
bent her dimpled knees and tucked
to sit down at her desk, we spoke in tongues.

Before FLYING OFF TO War

Before war, practice alms. Diplomas, awards
in fancy frames, anything with your name engraved,
give up. Take trophies to kids on the street
too skinny to win. Give away your coat,

both coats. Stock the pantry for your wife,
but haul your tools to a school, slum-side of town,
let them pick crowbars and hammers, drills, your awl,
your favorite cross saw. Donate your second car

to the Salvation Army, the March of Dimes—
it doesn't matter, and give them snow tires
you saved for a dazzling trip to Alaska.
Throw in the pup tent, your Boy Scout badges,

Grandfather's elk heads in the attic.
Give all black Bibles away but one. No,
hold nothing back. Even Saigon has chaplains.
Give up your wife, both children. Silently say goodbye

to Mother, Father far away. Haul out the trunk
and dump whatever's left. Drag it outside.
A truck from the Foundation for the Blind
comes by on Fridays. By Friday, you'll be gone.

UNCLE EARL'S LAST RIDE IN DALLAS

Uncle Earl's blue suit hung like a rustler's,
four pairs of boots lined up like a posse's
in the closet. We did what we must
with a will's stipulation—Levi's
and long-sleeved shirt unbuttoned,
his best beaver Stetson, back brim cut flush

to let his head lie flat. A chaw of Red Man
in his jaws, stitched tight and natural,
except no ooze, no chewing. Dress boots
were under there somewhere, although
no coffin would show them, polished or not.
But when they rolled the casket in, we heard

the jangle of spurs, muffled by the fluff
and satin. Old Earl would have been the first
to chortle, the way he hobbled off with his hat,
gored by the only bull to toss him in years,
a glove holding his ribs to hide the blood,
as if patting his chest pocket for a smoke.

some days nothing can save us

Once, when our son was four,
playing with cousins, he slammed
and stumbled into the house,
crying as if smashed by a rock.

Older kids told why, led us
to a dumpster in the alley
a few doors down. All had gone
exploring, peeking at trash
to see what treasures

neighbors had thrown away. Sometimes,
a day brings games and baubles;
sometimes, bricks and blood.
The shock of what Charles saw
was a fact I never learned
until Saigon, that some days

nothing can save us. Some fool
had killed blind kittens with a stone,
and for weeks they clawed
in his mind at night, kitten fur
and blood and bile, little teeth
like zippers that couldn't close.

ROCK SOFTLY IN MY ARMS

Forget the bells, the call to order
in assembly. High school is over,
boot camp a snipe hunt I survived.
The days of diapers and teen-age rage

are gone, flicked by
fast-forward on the VCR.
Now comes the time to hold coats
close to the throat in winter,

the stiff, clipped steps
on icy sidewalks, dark hours
in a chair before birds sing.
Come, clasp my stiff knuckles

at the fireplace, bifocals off
for an hour. Rock softly
in my arms and hold me, girl,
this night won't last for long.

ABOUT THE AUTHOR

Walt McDonald was named Texas Poet Laureate in 2001—one of many accomplishments in his extensive career. Among other honors he has received the Bookend Award for a lifetime of contributions to Texas literature from Texas Tech University Press in 2004, won four Western Heritage Awards from the National Cowboy Hall of Fame, the Spur Award from the Western Writers of America, and six awards from the Texas Institute of Letters, including the Lon Tinkle Memorial Award for Excellence Sustained Throughout a Career.

McDonald received a PhD from the University of Iowa and established the Creative Writing Department at Texas Tech University, retiring in May 2002 as a Paul Whitfield Horn Professor of English and Poet in Residence. Before entering academia fulltime, McDonald served in the United States Air Force in Vietnam. His experience as a pilot energizes many of his poems, but much of his work inhabits a recognizably Texan landscape—delving into ranch life, community, marriage, and raising children.

TCU Press honors Walt McDonald's remarkable career in this tenth book of the TCU Texas Poet Laureate Series.